Edjeane Alves Nunes
Lilian O. Ramires

WQC - WebQuest Collaborative

Edjeane Alves Nunes
Lilian O. Ramires

WQC - WebQuest Collaborative

A Collaborative WebQuest editor

ScienciaScripts

Imprint

Cover image: www.ingimage.com

This book is a translation from the original published under ISBN 978-3-330-99592-5.

Publisher:
Sciencia Scripts
is a trademark of
Dodo Books Indian Ocean Ltd. and OmniScriptum S.R.L publishing group

120 High Road, East Finchley, London, N2 9ED, United Kingdom
Str. Armeneasca 28/1, office 1, Chisinau MD-2012, Republic of Moldova, Europe
Managing Directors: Ieva Konstantinova, Victoria Ursu
info@omniscriptum.com

Printed at: see last page
ISBN: 978-620-8-58744-4

"The higher we rise, the smaller we seem in the eyes of those who cannot ***fly. "***

- Friedrich Wilhelm Nietzsche.

To my parents Edineuza Nunes Alves and José Alves Filho, for teaching me to walk on my own two feet and to fight for what I want, always doing the right thing. To my siblings Edneia Alves Nunes Sousa *(in memorian)* - with whom I would love to be able to share this moment - and José George Alves Nunes for their support. To my niece Bruna Maria Nunes Souza who allowed me to be her mum. To my fiancé Silvio André de Freitas Beserra for always being by my side at all times.

To the most important people in my life...

ACKNOWLEDGEMENTS

I would like to thank my course mates, especially José Guedes dos Santos Júnior and Leonardo de Lima Souza, for their friendship, companionship and, above all, their willingness to help anyone who needed it throughout the course.

I would like to thank my teachers, especially Lilian Oliveira Ramires and Glauber Maglhães Pires, my tutors, for their dedicated efforts and for the trust they placed in me. I would also like to thank Carlos André Batista for being a friend as well as a teacher.

Nobody achieves anything absolutely alone, thank you.

SUMMARY

CHAPTER 1

Introduction

With the advent of technology, various systems have been developed to make previously impossible tasks easier. In 1995, Bernie Dodge, a professor at San Diego State University, proposed that students develop an investigative task using mainly Internet resources. The methodological proposal was for a guided, investigative activity in which the subject matter was presented in a creative way (SILVA; FERRARI, 2006), which gave rise to the WebQuest (WQ). In the field of education, the WebQuest acts as a mediating methodology in the teaching-learning process, where the educator develops a kind of practical activity aimed at the learner in relation to certain content.

This activity is structurally made up of seven parts: introduction, task, resources, process, evaluation, conclusion and credits. Each part of the WebQuest guides the learner step by step through the proposed task, respectively presenting a brief introduction to the topic covered; the activity to be carried out; the suggested resources (research sources); the stages in the development of the work; the assessment process; the importance of studying this topic and the references used during the making of the WebQuest.

The methodology mentioned above has been growing and reaching more and more educators who are looking to make their classes more dynamic, encourage teamwork and spread the use of technology in education (SILVA; FERRARI, 2006). Its proposal involves the use of collaboration in the development of classroom tasks and, based on the conviction that "we learn more and better with others than alone" (DODGE, 1995), this process becomes more efficient.

Some learning theories associated with WebQuest make it even more relevant when it comes to collaborative activities. The social interactionist theory, for example, has a lot to contribute in this respect. In this theory, Vygotsky (1989) cites learning as "[...] a social process in which subjects construct their knowledge through their interaction with the environment and with others".

In this way, WebQuest mediates the teaching-learning process and makes use of collaborative work as a way of overcoming difficulties in this process and shortening positive results in this regard.

The use of this activity in the classroom has emerged as a didactic alternative for educators, because making lessons more dynamic is a constant need in teachers' routines, and always managing to develop a creative way of presenting content is a challenge that most often requires the use of technology and innovative tools.

In this way, this work aims to develop an easy-to-use WebQuest editor that meets the needs of teachers and students in relation to research activities carried out collectively, acting as an intervener in the process of constructing the tasks proposed by the teacher, striving for objectivity and clarity in its composition and guiding students through the research process from reliable research sources.

This work has five chapters: Introduction, Theoretical Framework, Methodology, WQC - WebQuest Collaborative and Conclusion. The Introduction has two sections - objectives and justification. The Theoretical Framework has five sections - WebQuest (with the subsection Collaborative work), Cognitive Load Theory (with the subsection Usability), Learning theories, Related work (showing three works) and a brief summary of the chapter. The WQC - WebQuest Collaborative chapter presents the WQC tool. Finally, the Conclusion chapter.

1.2 Objectives

The general aim of this work is to enable educators to use a WebQuest editor, built on a standard structure, optimising group activities, making them clear and objective and encouraging teacher creativity.

The specific objectives of this work are:

F Carry out a requirements assessment with the help of educators;

- Analysing requirements to better recognise the problem;
- Define the system architecture;
- Implement the system;
- Carry out checks.

1.3 Justification

With the advance of technology and the spread of the means of communication, there is an increasing need to produce and use documents digitally and in a shared way, for reasons of practicality and, above all, efficiency. In the historical context, the degree of importance represented by this evolution, which emerged with the computer age, reinforces the importance of investing in the creation and improvement of instruments that fulfil these tasks.

The WebQuest editor is a clear example of this type of tool. And, due to the difficulties encountered by educators in using technological resources and/or developing electronic pages (NETO et al., 2014), the construction of an easy-to-use editor has emerged as an alternative to make the activities proposed in the classroom fun, as well as clear and objective, so that the presentation of the content is more attractive for both the students and the teacher and without requiring too much practical or theoretical knowledge from the users of this system.

WQC - WebQuest Collaborative arose from the need to incorporate the use of technology into classrooms in a targeted and efficient way, providing teachers with a simple interface and an editing area with tools similar to those found in the most commonly used text editors, increasing practicality in the formatting process, reducing the complexity of making WebQuests and consequently the work of the authors. Another factor to consider is that there are few systems similar to this, available free of charge and mainly with usable interfaces in Portuguese.

The use of Information and Communication Technologies (ICT), associated with learning theories, favours the construction of knowledge at any level of education (CARDOSO; BORGES, 2013). However, according to Sancho (2006), one of the main obstacles for schools and teachers is precisely knowing how to exploit the potential of this set of technologies, in other words, "recognising and adopting educational visions that make it possible to rethink the role of students, knowledge, assessment and the educational community in improving teaching and learning processes".

In this context, Cardoso and Borges (2013) state that WebQuest is a pedagogical strategy for interaction, complementing content, deepening themes and also an auxiliary activity in the formation of a more autonomous, questioning, critical, creative student and producer of new knowledge. According to Delors et al. (1996), this methodology seeks to revive the importance of research as an attitude to help students achieve scientific knowledge in a process where they gradually learn to select data.

In their paper, Bottentuit Junior and Coutinho (2010) present the results of two pedagogical experiments developed in higher education using the WebQuest methodology. The samples were made up of students from two classes with different activity proposals:

- in the first class with 34 (thirty-four) students, only 6% (two students) had already used this methodology. With regard to their opinion of the WebQuest strategy, 88% considered that learning was more fun, 76% said they had learnt without the teacher's help, 56% reported that they had learnt to use the Internet more efficiently and 68% had learnt to search the web;
- In the second class, 56 (sixty-six) students completed the research, of whom 85% said they had learnt new ways of teaching and learning using web resources and only 9% did not consider the WebQuest pedagogical proposal to be very effective, 80% reported having learnt to value the team's ideas and 78% said they had worked collaboratively, 70% said they had learnt to look for other sources of research on the web, while 67% said they had exercised creativity and 63% were satisfied with the final work.

This work was motivated by the existing demand for the use of information technologies in an academic environment, encouraging teacher creativity, disseminating technological resources to learners and optimising group activities by previously specifying the objective of the proposed activities and listing the most important points for their implementation.

CHAPTER 2

Theoretical Framework

This chapter discusses the main topics involved in developing the project, divided into three sections. These include the WebQuest section, which is analysed in terms of its importance and dissemination, and also includes a subsection on Collaborative Work; the Usability section, with the Cognitive Load Theory subsection; the Learning Theories section, which lists the main theories related to WebQuest; and finally the Related Work section, which presents three works that have a relevant correlation with the theme of the project.

2.1 The WebQuest

The term WebQuest was defined in 1995 by Bernie Dodge, a professor at San Diego State University (SILVA; FERRARI, 2009) and according to Bottentuit Junior and Coutinho (2010) the term is etymologically the sum of two words, Web (network of hyperlinks) and Quest (questioning, search or research). According to Dodge (1996) WebQuest is a guided enquiry in which some or all of the information with which learners interact comes from Internet resources, optionally supplemented with videoconferences, chats, forums, electronic mail and the use of other means of producing collaborative writing, such as wiki, blogs, etc.

Bottentuit Junior and Coutinho (2010) define the Internet as a huge conglomerate of easily and quickly accessible information, available in various formats and from a wide variety of sources, constantly changing and growing exponentially. Thus, according to Silva and Ferrari (2009), the WebQuest methodology presents an activity in an attractive way and with a defined direction based on the subject covered. Thus, this technique avoids so-called "surfing" the net without a clear task in mind and prevents plagiarism, increasing student productivity by specifying guidelines to be followed and recommending bibliographical references.

According to Bottentuit Junior and Coutinho (2010) it is necessary for educators to reflect on the use of web resources by students, considering strategies that lead students to convert information into knowledge and not to mechanise the reproduction of content found on the web. In this way, according to Bottentuit Junior and Coutinho (2010), research-orientated tactics on the web take on a significant degree of importance in the teaching-learning process, mainly due to the huge range of content of dubious origin and/or without scientific proof published indiscriminately. In this context, the WebQuest emerges as a guiding tool to be proposed by the teacher and used by the students to support their research.

There are two levels of WebQuest to be distinguished from each other, short WebQuest and long WebQuest. According to Dodge (1996), the first level deals with the acquisition and integration of knowledge and is designed to be completed in one to three lessons, while the second level comprises the expansion and refinement of knowledge and takes between a week and a month to complete. It should be noted that regardless of which level the WebQuest is at, it will always be designed to optimise the learner's time while carrying out the proposed activity.

According to Dodge (1995), Bottentuit Junior and Coutinho (2010), in order to achieve the efficiency and clarity mentioned above, the WebQuest must be structured with at least the following parts:

- Introduction - presenting information about the content in question, instigating the student's curiosity and underpinning the research process;
- Task - clearly describing an action (it must be challenging and executable);
- Resources - pointing out sources of information that make it possible to complete the work;
- Process - presenting the description of the steps to carry out the proposed task;
- Assessment - explaining to students how the activity will be assessed;
- Conclusion - summarising the general purpose of what has been learned and indicating ways in which the student can continue to study the subject;
- Credits - providing references to the authors of the WebQuest, the sources of the figures or texts used (important information).

According to Silva and Ferrari (2009), collaboration is also part of the proposal to use WebQuest, where everyone involved exchanges information and shares experiences. According to Dodge (1995), WebQuest is based on the premise that learning is more effective in groups than working individually, and thus the expressiveness of learning is the result of collaboration between those involved. Silva and Ferrari (2009) also state that it is up to teachers to use WebQuest in such a way that, in addition to its wide-ranging possibilities, it allows students to work in teams and consequently exchange knowledge between these participants.

The task proposed by the educators must therefore have an investigative nature and the solution must be based on the collaborative work of each team. Because the real aim of the methodology adopted (WebQuest) is to encourage teams to work entirely collaboratively, leaving competitiveness to one side in order to always seek results collectively and not just co-operatively, i.e. all the members develop the solution together and not just a fraction of it.

2.1.1 Collaborative work

According to Franco (2003), the increased complexity of the routines experienced in today's world is increasingly demanding greater interaction between people.
In this way, carrying out activities in groups of people in a way that is not only collaborative, but also co-operative, through an environment and via the Internet, has become more than a necessity. According to Zank (2010), teamwork has advantages that go beyond the competitiveness of organisations and, although these advantages are unquestionable, they are not the only ones to be taken into account.

The demand to work collectively aroused the teams' interest in doing so in a way that wasted less time on travelling or even on having a place that could accommodate all the group members. Computer-supported collaborative work enters this context as a facilitator, breaking down physical and time barriers. According to Alonso et al. (2003) the new paradigms technological point to emerging needs for the educational process and other professional activities, especially with regard to the development of collaborative work.

Franco (2003) states that when collaborative work is done correctly, it significantly increases quality, efficiency and reduces the time spent carrying out various tasks. According to Dodge (1996), every Webquest involves tasks in groups, and these groups work towards achieving a single goal. Therefore, learning from shared knowledge is fundamental.

2.2 Cognitive Load Theory

According to Santos and Tarouco (2007), the development of educational systems requires the adoption of metrics that act to make the resource more efficient, meeting the human cognitive process and contributing quality to the learning process. In this way, the Cognitive Load Theory emphasises that in the use of technological solutions, the quality of the learning resources, the situations that are created and the environments that are developed are essential factors for expanding the learning process, student involvement and capacity for interaction.

The Cognitive Load Theory is due to John Sweller, an Australian psychologist, who dedicated himself to studying this theory (SANTOS; TAROUCO, 2007). According to Santos and Tarouco (2007), Cognitive Load Theory is a universal set of principles that result in an efficient learning environment and that consequently promote an increase in the capacity of the human cognition process. According to Tarouco and Cunha (2006) these principles aim to make human interaction with technology more aligned with the cognitive process.

Santos and Tarouco (2007) stress that given the volume of information, interaction resources, animation, sounds and colours, which are often part of the solutions used in education, it is important to have a broader understanding of the human cognitive process and how Cognitive Load Theory can help enhance learning.

According to Tarouco and Cunha (2006), a screen with a complex or unconventional design that uses different fonts, objects, navigation tools and layout patterns will generally have a high procedural or functional cognitive load because each component will need to be perceived and interpreted by the learner. In contrast, Santos and Tarouco (2007) state that an appropriate learning environment, following the principles of Cognitive Load Theory, minimises unnecessary mental resources, thus maximising learning.

According to Santos and Tarouco (2007), this theory encompasses all types of content and media in order to enhance learning and develop flexible skills through the creation and use of learning resources and environments that are in tune with the human cognitive process.

Tarouco and Cunha (2006) point out that educational materials in digital media, as well as learning objects, often overload learners' working memory. They also emphasise that learning is not just about identifying concepts, but about understanding what has been worked on, and stress that, according to the Cognitive Load Theory, it is naturally impossible for human beings to process a lot of information in their memory at any one time.

According to Santos and Tarouco (2007 apud MAYER, 2001) some forms of cognitive load are considered useful, while others waste mental resources. Thus, when designing content for teaching materials, the three main types of cognitive load are considered:

- Intrinsic cognitive load - imposed by the complexity of the content of the teaching material;
- Natural (relevant) cognitive load - imposed by teaching activities that benefit the learning objective;
- Cognitive load external to the content (irrelevant) - does not interfere with the construction and automation of schemas, and consequently wastes limited mental resources that could be used to assist the natural load.

For the learning process to reach a good level of efficiency, according to Santos and Tarouco (2007), it is necessary to balance these loads, as shown in Figure 2.1.

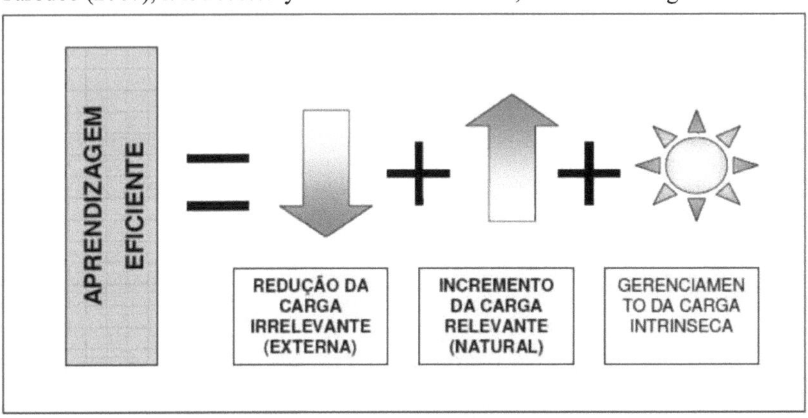

Figure 2.1 - Cognitive Load Balancing Model
Source: Model adapted from Mayer (2001b)

In relation to the model shown in Figure 2.1, Santos and Tarouco (2007) point out that when you can't control the intrinsic load associated with the learning objectives, you can control it by segmenting and sequencing the content in a way that optimises the number of interactive elements at any one time.

The Cognitive Load Theory argues that the development of teaching materials, especially those that use multimedia, should follow certain principles in order to reduce the student's cognitive overload and enhance their learning (SANTOS; TAROUCO, 2007). The principles defended by this theory are:

- Principle of Multiple Representation: students learn better when words and images are combined than when words alone are used.
- Principle of Spatial Proximity: this principle concerns the proximity of words and images, i.e. when corresponding words and images are close together rather than far apart.
- Principle of Non-Division or Temporal Proximity: this principle involves presenting words and images simultaneously rather than successively, since presenting a text and an animation on the same screen in succession divides the student's attention.
- Principle of Individual Differences: it is known that students with a higher level of knowledge about a given subject and a greater degree of spatial orientation are better able to organise and process their own knowledge when interacting with the subject.
- Coherence Principle: refers to the exclusion of words, images or sounds that are not relevant to the subject. The simpler and more objective the presentation of the content, the freer the working memory will be to process a greater amount of knowledge.
- Principle of Redundancy: this principle emphasises that the use of animation and narration, when used simultaneously in the teaching process, enhances knowledge, unlike when used separately.

These principles were developed by Richard Mayer, a research professor at the University of California, Santa Barbara, following on from research into Sweller's Cognitive Load Theory, and have been shown to minimise cognitive overload, thus enhancing the cognitive learning process (SANTOS; TAROUCO, 2007).

Santos and Tarouco (2007) point to studies showing that cognitive load is an ever-present factor in human computer interaction, as each element on the screen must be interpreted by the user and consequently takes up some of the user's mental energy. Tarouco and Cunha (2007) also stress the importance of knowing how to choose a resource that presents a reduced load and can maximise the processing of the knowledge being taught.

Santos and Tarouco (2007) cite recent studies showing that the human cognition system has independent inputs for visual and verbal information. In other words, by making use of two independent perception channels in the teaching and learning process, the cognitive load can be reduced, as long as the information is not redundant, otherwise the cognitive load increases. The use of two channels is considered effective when they have complementary objectives.

Santos and Tarouco (2007) add that the aim of a good layout for educational use is to reduce the amount of energy directed towards interacting with the system, thus freeing up cognitive capacity to process what is being taught. Because interactivity means that various elements of knowledge have to be coordinated in the student's memory in order to carry out a series of activities, and this can cause overload.

2.2.1 Usability

A usable interface is an essential requirement in the presentation of an information system. Considering that the execution of software processes most often requires some kind of interaction with the interface and that the user's performance depends on this contact, it is possible to realise that the system is strongly evaluated by the way the interface is presented to the end user.

According to Nielsen and Loranger (2007), usability integrates multiple components and applies to all aspects of a system with which the user has to interact, including installation and maintenance. It is related to the ease of use of something, quantified by quality attributes and directly related to the interface. Cybis et al. (2010) adds that usability is the attribute that characterises the use of an interactive system. Thus, according to Nielsen and Loranger (2007), the quality of user interaction with a given interface is associated with the following principles:

- ease of learning;
- ease of remembering how to perform a task after some time;
- speed in carrying out tasks;
- low error rate;

- subjective user satisfaction.

According to Nielsen and Loranger (2007), the interface has a usability problem when a particular user or group of users finds it difficult to: carry out a task with the interface, find the desired information on the site, return to a previously visited page, etc. The occurrence of links containing invalid URLs is also a relevant fault. Problems of this kind can lead to data loss, reduced productivity and even user rejection of the software.

The inappropriate use of multimedia resources is also a usability problem, such as the abusive use of too many colours in the same environment, as well as when background and text colours are not chosen appropriately. These factors can make the page unreadable and/or cause visual fatigue and divert the user's attention. Given this scenario, according to Winckler and Pimenta (2002) some metrics should be observed, such as:

- User performance during task completion: analysing task completion (successful, partially completed, not completed), task completion time (when long, this may indicate unnecessary user effort), error occurrence (caused by a user operation and induced by the interface or by a system activity, in the latter case there should be a warning issued by the software and support offered to recover from the error);
- Subjective user satisfaction: usability is considered subjective, each user has their own individual needs and satisfying these minimises any problems related to the interface;
- Correspondence with the user's objectives: this can be a quantitative or qualitative metric, checking whether the users' final objective has been achieved;
- Adherence to standards (norms, ergonomic recommendations, etc.): these can prevent or reduce various usability problems, such as the ergonomic norms and recommendations defined by ISO9241.

Usability problems are in fact identified during use of the interface. Winckler and Pimenta (2002), among other authors, state that the process of developing usable interfaces is a continuous cycle of design and evaluation. Evaluations can be carried out using a prototype and the method used varies according to the stage of development. The cycle ends when no usability problems have been identified and/or the most serious problems have been solved.

It is of the utmost importance to assign each usability problem a degree of severity, so that the most important problems that require an immediate solution are prioritised. In this way, the degree of severity can be assessed in relation to the impact on the performance of tasks and the frequency with which the problem occurs (WOOLRYCH; COCKTON, 2001).

With regard to impact, the degree of severity of usability problems can be classified into three categories according to Winckler and Pimenta (2002):

- Serious: users do not complete the task (spend more than two minutes);
- Important: users successfully complete the task (they spend up to two minutes);
- Minor impact: users encounter the problem, get round it without jeopardising the quality of the task.

With regard to frequency (scale with five users participating in the evaluation), the degree of severity of usability problems, according to Winckler and Pimenta (2002), is classified as:

- High frequency: problems occur with more than three users;
- Medium frequency: problems occur with two or three users;
- Low frequency: problems occur with only one user.

In this way, the concept of usability requires a more in-depth analysis of certain aspects. According to Santos and Tarouco (2007) in the use of technologies in education, the quality of the learning resources, the situations that are created and the environments that are developed are essential for expanding the learning process, the involvement and the ability of students to interact with the learning objects. According to Tarouco and Cunha (2006), learning objects are a new type of computer-based instruction that can be reused in different learning contexts.

According to Santos and Tarouco (2007), a large number of technological and media resources are available to education, but many of these resources do not add quality to the teaching-learning process and end up confusing, discouraging or even distracting students. Therefore, choosing or developing a technological resource that meets the needs required for a good education becomes a challenge for everyone involved.

Tarouco and Cunha (2006) therefore emphasise that it is necessary to consider the appropriate way of combining the various types of media that technology currently requires according to the way in which the cognition process takes place.

According to Tarouco and Cunha (2006) a screen that uses standard conventions in the text, graphics, navigation and layout will be easier to interpret and consequently will have a much lower cognitive load. Santos and Tarouco (2007) define cognitive load as an understandable set of principles that form the Cognitive Load Theory.

2.3 Learning theories

Various theories have been defined throughout history with regard to the learning process, and multiple authors have brought these conceptions together in their research in isolation and/or together according to the relationship between them. Some of these theories will be discussed in this section according to their correlation with the WebQuest teaching methodology.

According to Vygostsky (1989), learning is more effective when the proposed activities present a cognitive challenge. The author also emphasises that tasks need to provide learners with the means to deepen their knowledge, based on previous knowledge and exchanges with colleagues through collaborative learning. Thus, WebQuest can be inserted into this context, considering that according to Dodge (1996), every WebQuest involves tasks in groups, with the aim of achieving a single objective.

According to Santos (2012), when referring to the use of WebQuest in the teaching-learning process, it is necessary to consider the construction of knowledge through a Vygotskyan paradigm, the concept of Zone of Proximal Development (ZDP), introduced by Vygotsky in the socio-historical theory and referenced by Abar and Barbosa (2008) as fundamental and strictly related to the WebQuest methodology.

Passerino and Santarosa (2000) define the ZDP well, classifying it as collective (social), because several individuals (learner participants) interact and construct knowledge together, learning through the construction of shared representations through the use of instruments. In a broader analysis, Vygotsky (1998) states that there are two levels of development of the subject, real development (what they actually know and master), called the Zone of Real Development (ZDR) and proximal development (potential that the subject may develop depending on the social context in which they are immersed), called the Zone of Proximal Development (ZDP).

Santos (2012) states that in the school environment, the ZDP acts in a direct way, as it seeks to shape the social character of human development based on the historical-cultural mediations of each individual. Passerino and Santarosa (2000) state that this concept emerged to better explain the relationship between external (inter) and internal (intra) processes and is closely related to the Higher Psychological Processes (HPS), since it is in the ZDP that the HPS development process takes place. Vygotsky defines these processes as mental functions that characterise conscious human behaviour.

In their specific studies on learning, Neves and Damiani (2006) cite Lev Vygotsky's socio-historical theory, which treats learning as an internal, active and interpersonal process - in contrast to the ideas in force at the time of its conception. This theory sees learning not as the mere acquisition of information, or as something that happens from a simple association of ideas stored in the memory.

According to Passerino and Santarosa (2000), Information Technology in Education, with regard to the construction of computer environments for educational use, has been influenced by these two epistemological currents. The first emphasises the transmission of information and the second sees the computer as a mediating instrument for the student to construct knowledge. In this way, these currents are responsible for the way in which technology is introduced into the teaching and learning process.

According to Passerino and Santarosa (2000), these currents group epistemological theories according to their conception of the subject-object relationship and the concept of learning behind this relationship. Similar to socio-historical theory, as well as WebQuest, the constructionist current makes it possible to establish relationships that arise through the interaction and participation of its members in collective activities. To the detriment of this aspect, Passerino and Santarosa (2000) state that this "participation/interaction" presupposes accepting rules that specify a goal to be achieved, as well as establishing the idea of collectivity among group members, while at the same time providing greater autonomy for participants.

2.4 Related work

Some related work was found and analysed in order to predict the real need for the development of a WebQuest editor that would improve on the models already built.

2.4.1 WebQuest as a didactic activity that enhances education

The work by Silva and Ferrari (2009) describes the WebQuest methodology, emphasising the use of this tool and the technological resources available online for the construction of networked knowledge, highlighting the need for reflection on the pure and simple use of solutions in the field of technology (which methodologies to use and what they can offer). In this sense, the role of educators who use technology in their classes is to avoid using it in a coercive and exclusionary way, restricting student autonomy. It is therefore important to be more open to this world of possibilities, adding potential to lessons.

Figure 2.2 - WebQuest Virtual Newspaper home screen
Source: Fernanda Quaresma da Silva and Hélio Oliveira Ferrari (2009)

Abar and Barbosa (2008) present seven topics for the structure of a WebQuest: introduction, task, resources, process, evaluation, conclusion and credits. All of these topics are fundamental for the WebQuest to follow the standards suggested by Dodge, . However, in the work of Silva and Ferrari (2009), based on the theme worked on, an adaptation to the original model was made, as can be seen in Figure 2.2.

The example of a WebQuest proposed in Silva and Ferrari's work (2009) is the "Virtual Newspaper", which was used as a teaching resource with students in the 6th grade of a public school in Uberlândia - MG. The strategy used was based on the students' previous knowledge, the exchange of knowledge, collective work (emphasising its relevance) and conversation circles between students and educators.

The "Virtual Newspaper" arose from the need to enhance the "Newspaper" project (worked on previously) and the aim was to build a WebQuest in order to make the proposal more attractive by creating a newspaper on the Web. The idea was to create it in a text or HTML editor. As the students were already familiar with Word and Publisher, these tools were chosen.

The article presents points in common with the project under development, in terms of the application of WebQuest in the classroom with teachers and students, using the educator as the central mediator of the teaching-learning process. In terms of structure, it was noted that some of the topics defined by Dodge as the standard for WebQuest were adapted to the work, diverging from the project in question on this point. As far as development is concerned, specific text (Word) and HTML (Publisher) editors were used, which is also in line with the methodology proposed in the project under development.

2.4.2 Webquester: Tool for Creating WebQuests with Online Assessments

Vieira's work (2008) presents the development of the tool ("Webquester"). This tool allows a teacher to create dynamic websites via a *web* browser and carry out online assessments using pre-programmed templates following the methodology created by Dodge (WebQuest).

The "Webquester" tool allows a bank of questions to be created, as can be seen in Figure 2.3, where they can be reused in other online assessments integrated with WebQuests. WebQuests created using this system remain available to anyone who wishes to access them. However, the online assessments associated with the WebQuest have restricted access to the group of students for whom the assessment is intended and to the author of the WebQuest, via a unique password generated by the teacher during the process of preparing each assessment.

Figura 2.3 - WebQuests home screen on Webquester
Source: Yauari Vieira (2008)

The tool is developed in the Hypertext Preprocessor (PHP) programming language in its fifth version, as the authors believe it offers considerable performance, good support for Object Orientation (OO) and a vast community of developers and consultation materials available on the web. The database management system used is My Structured Query Language (MySQL) because it is open source and the most widely used with PHP, as well as offering satisfactory performance for the intended application.

With regard to the structure of WebQuests, the author cites the use of seven sections by convention defined according to Dodge: introduction, task, process, sources of information or resources, evaluation, conclusion and credits. The author also presents other systems (related works) that deviate from this standard, with fewer or mixed sections according to the need encountered during the creation of his WebQuest.

The "WebQuester" development stage starts with a survey of Functional Requirements (FR) and Non-Functional Requirements (NFR), and continues with the diagrams (Use Case Diagrams, Class Diagrams, three sequence diagrams showing the main processes of the tool and the Entity Relational Diagram, showing the organisation of the data in the database). The tool used for implementation (programming and integration of the technologies used) was Zend Studio (ZEND, 2007). One limitation of the Zend tool was identified.

As far as the techniques and tools used in the implementation are concerned, Cascading Style Sheets (CSS) as a mechanism for adding styles to web documents (font, colours, etc.); ClassGenerator as an auxiliary tool (developed by the author himself) that creates the necessary codes in PHP (code generator); jQuery as an AJAX framework and also a framework for the JavaScript language (code generator).); ClassGenerator as an auxiliary tool (developed by the project author himself) that creates the necessary codes in the PHP language (code generator); jQuery as an AJAX framework and also a framework for the JavaScript language (which is why it was chosen, as well as simplifying JavaScript code); the What You See Is What You Get (WYSIWYG) Editor as a resource that serves to replace the standard multi-line text input fields with functionalities (inserting images, links, etc.).

As jQuery is open source, it has a large number of plugins available. In this work, two of these plugins were used: Masked Input, which is used to mask data input fields, allowing, for example, the creation of date and number patterns (DIGITAL BUSH, 2008) and Suggest, which is used to create suggestions for filling in text fields based on the incomplete texts in these fields.

The author concludes by pointing out some of the deficiencies found in the related tools studied throughout the project, highlighting the language criterion as the main obstacle when using these tools, classifying the translations as poor or incomplete. He analyses as a positive factor the fact that "Webquester" is available completely in Portuguese and free of charge, as well as having an online evaluation feature.

The work presented in this subsection bears a significant resemblance to the project under development. It is possible to see several characteristics in common between the two, especially with regard to the development of the tools themselves. The initial compatibility of is the use of CSS, jQuery, MySQL and PHP. The main difference is that Webquester has an online evaluation function.

2.4.3 WQE: A Versatile WebQuest Editor

The work carried out by Camargo and Fernandes (2010) presents the construction of the WebQuest editor WQE, an acronym for WebQuest Editor, which allows WebQuests to be generated in the format of the IMS *Learning Design* - IMSLD standard, a standard that contains a metalanguage for constructing learning units, free of pedagogical methods (IMS, 2003), in order to facilitate the creation of WebQuests in the context of *Learning Management* Systems (LMS). WQE can also be used outside the context of LMSs, in HTML format.

IMS is a non-profit organisation that strives to enable the growth and impact of learning technology in the education and corporate learning sectors worldwide. Its main activity is the development of interoperability standards and standards of practice for the adoption of distributed learning, some of which are learning interoperability tools (IMS, 2003).

As a reference scenario for the use of WebQuests, this work emphasises the definition of the ideal tool for editing WebQuests, where the main actor is an instructor with the aim of creating WebQuests and using them without worrying about technical issues when designing an instructional activity, generating activities that can be used in various formats (printed on paper, published on the Internet or used in the context of an LMS). In this way, the educator will only be concerned with the pedagogical strategy, instructional objectives and content.

The WQE is structured to allow the creation of WebQuests in accordance with the IMSLD specification and taking into account the definitions set by Dodge, as can be seen in Figure 2.4. To do this, an IMSLD mapping for WebQuests was developed and a basic mould was created, making it possible to edit learning activities, where each activity corresponds to a WebQuest section.

WQE is the first editor of WebQuests (to our knowledge) according to the IMSLD standard in the literature. It was designed for authoring WebQuests, in the context of a specific LMS or independently (CAMARGO; FERNANDES, 2010). Experiments were carried out with students and planned with authors (teachers) for a future application.

The WQE WebQuest editor correlates with the editor proposed in this work in terms of WebQuests made available in HTML and the adoption of the standard defined by Dodge for this methodology, but it distances itself from the context when it follows the IMSLD specifications, which are not addressed in this project.

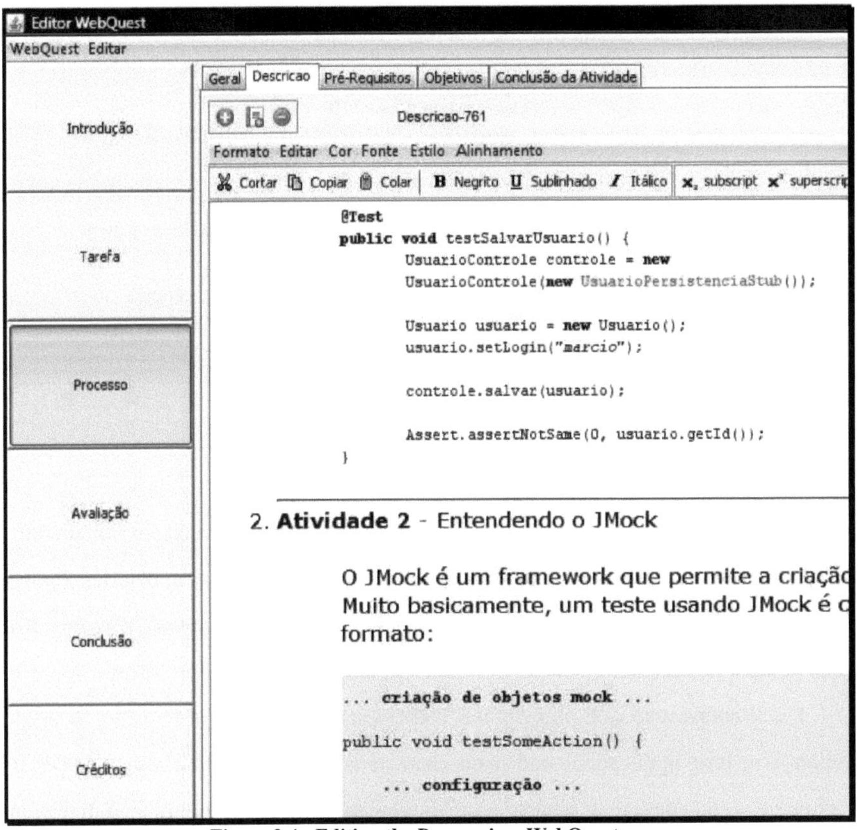

Figure 2.4 - Editing the Process in a WebQuest screen

Source: Elisa Zaroni Camargo and Clovis Torres Fernandes (2010)

2.4.4 Comparative analysis of related work

The related works were chosen on the basis of identifying common characteristics with the work developed. Table 2.1 shows a brief comparative analysis of these works in relation to the editor built, showing both the points that correspond and the points that differ.

Table 2.1 - Comparative analysis of related works

RELATED WORK	FEATURES	
	CORRELATION	DISTINCTIONS
WebQuest as a teaching activity.	- Use of WQ in classrooms; - WebQuests available in HTML.	- Bemie Dodge pattern adapted; - Development using specific text (Word) and HTML (Publisher) editors;

Webquester: A Tool for Creating WebQuests with Online Assessments.	- Bemie Dodge pattern; - Use of WQ in classrooms; - Development using CSS, jQuery, MySQL and PHP; - WebQuests available in HTML.	- It has *online* reviews,
WQE: a Versatile WebQuest Editor.	- Bemie Dodge standard (adopts two models); - Use of WQ in classrooms; - WebQuests available in HTML.	- Bemie Dodge pattern adapted; - Follow IMSLD specifications;

Source: Prepared by the author

2.5 Chapter summary

This chapter presents five sections: The WebQuest (with the subsection Collaborative works), Cognitive Load Theory (with the subsection Usability), Learning theories, Related works (presenting three works) and a brief summary of the chapter exposing a comparative analysis of the works related to the project under development.

The WebQuest section presents the WebQuest methodology in terms of its origin, definition, structure, applications and main characteristics. This section also includes the Collaborative work subsection, which describes how to carry out work collaboratively and the advantages over work carried out individually.

The second section deals with the Cognitive Load Theory, setting out the principles defined in the theory, the correlation of each of them with the human cognitive process and their application in the development of usable interfaces. The section also sets out the Usability subsection, which deals with usability principles and the quality of user interaction, usability problems, metrics to be applied and the degree of severity of usability errors.

The next section, Learning theories, presents theories associated with the WebQuest methodology, including Lev Vygotsky's socio-historical theory, which mentions the Zone of Proximal Development (ZDP), instructionism, which emphasises the transmission of information, and constructionism, which sees the computer as a mediating tool for the student to construct knowledge.

The last section presents three related works analysed and compared with WQC -

WebQuest Collaborative in Table 2.1. The analysis presents the characteristics common to the editor developed and the distinct points identified in the tools.

CHAPTER 3

Methodology

The project is carried out in five incremental stages: study of the topic, requirements gathering, analysis, implementation and verification tests. The initial stage is necessary to get to know the topic, relating it to the best possible form of presentation to increase student retention of the content and facilitate the teacher's work when creating the activity. Development begins with a survey of Functional Requirements (FR) and Non-Functional Requirements (NFR), carried out with the collaboration of a consultant teacher together with the developer, based on an interview aimed at the difficulties encountered in the classroom in relation to presenting content in an attractive way. Based on these requirements, the analysis stage begins, where the system is moulded and built to meet the defined specifications. The next step is implementation, where the requirements are revised as the stage progresses and tests are carried out.

The project is implemented using the Eclipse Integrated Development Environment (IDE), which is the most widely used IDE in the world (CAELUM, 2015) and is also a tool that follows the open source model of software development.

This stage continues using HTML5 (HyperText Markup Language), a language for structuring and presenting content. This version was chosen because it is the most up-to-date and because it brings with it important changes to the role of HTML in the world of the web, through new functionalities such as semantics and accessibility. The project also uses CSS3 (Cascading Style Sheets), a simple mechanism for defining styles for web pages with transition effects, images, fonts, formatting, colours and others, which give Web 2.0 pages a new style in all aspects of layout design. The use of CSS3 is due to the fact that it facilitates the development of work, due to the variety of transformations in the presentation of a website that this mechanism offers.

The programming language used to develop the system was PHP, a language that allows dynamic websites to be created, enabling interaction with the user through forms, URL (Uniform Resource Locator) parameters and links. It also has support for a large number of databases, such as dBase, Interbase, mSQL, mySQL, Oracle, Sybase, PostgreSQL and others (BARRETO, 2000). JavaScript, currently the main language for programming in web browsers according to Barreto (2000), was used to implement the client-side (client-server).

The project's architecture uses the DAO (Data Access Object) and VO (Value Object) design patterns, the database management system used is MySQL, because it is one of the most important relational databases, as well as being free and easy to install for all operating systems, and the XAMPP web server, because it is free, easy to use and capable of interpreting dynamic pages. It also uses the CKEditor plugin, a ready-to-use HTML text editor designed to simplify the creation of web content.

The final stage of the project's development involves the use of empirical tests verifying the RFs raised by the consultant professor together with the project developer. The tests aim to analyse the system as a whole in relation to meeting the predetermined specifications, so the quantification of the results obtained will be noted according to the efficiency observed in the diagnosis issued at each point analysed. In this way, the development process moves on to the next stage or back to the previous one until the specification is fully met.

Verification is an activity that involves analysing a system to make sure it meets functional and non-functional requirements. Thus, in the Requirements Testing technique applied, each functional requirement in the requirements document is analysed and a test is defined so that it can objectively ascertain whether the system satisfies the requirement. A test log table is filled in with the necessary information for each item tested, including the following information: identifier and name of requirements - one for each requirement, related requirements, test objective, technique, finalisation criteria and special considerations, as can be seen in APPENDIX B - Requirements Verification.

3.1 Validation plan

The validation plan corresponds to the steps to be followed during the system validation process, which will be carried out in future work, based on data collection from a sample of 5 educators.

In the first stage of validation, the teachers will be given a lecture on the central theme to be validated (WebQuest). After the lecture, the educators who took part in the lecture will be given time to mature their ideas on a possible subject to be covered using WebQuest. The next stage will be of a practical nature, where the sample mentioned above will use the WQC WebQuest editor, initially under a brief orientation on how the software works and once the WQC recognition stage has been completed, the educators will develop their own WebQuest under the observation of the project developer. The final stage is the application of a questionnaire, consisting of objective questions and a space for suggestions, focussing on the use of the system during the development of the WebQuest.

The data collected from the questionnaires will be analysed in relation to the system as a whole and in terms of compliance with the predetermined specifications, and the quantification of the results obtained will be noted according to the efficiency observed in the diagnosis issued at each point analysed.

CHAPTER 4

WQC - WebQuest Collaborative

The WebQuest editor WQC - WebQuest Collaborative was developed on the web platform and has a simple and effective interface for what it does. The tool makes it possible to create, edit and remove WebQuests in each session that is started. It also allows each user to generate a list of the WebQuests they have saved in the database via a search.

4.1 Software artefacts

The development of the WebQuest editor was based on the following software artefacts: functional requirements, non-functional requirements, use case diagram, ER model (with the tables that make up the database), class diagram and component diagram.

4.1.1 Functional Requirements

The specification of functional requirements was carried out with the help of a consultant teacher, based on the needs encountered in the classroom with regard to presenting content in a creative and efficient way, using technological resources and research on the World Wide Web.

RF. 01: Register user

The WebQuest editor will allow visitors to register and become users with free access to the system. Registration consists of your full name, e-mail address and unique password.

RF. 02: Create the WebQuest Theme

Registered users define a theme or subject for each WebQuest they create.

RF. 03: Create the Introduction stage of the WebQuest

Registered users define an introduction for each WebQuest they create.

RF. 04: Create the WebQuest Task step

Registered users define a task for each WebQuest created.

RF. 05: Create the WebQuest Resources step

Registered users define resources for each WebQuest created.

RF. 06: Create the WebQuest Process step

Registered users define a process for each WebQuest created.

RF. 07: Create the WebQuest Evaluation step

Registered users define a rating for each WebQuest they create.

RF. 08: Create the WebQuest Completion step

Registered users define a conclusion for each WebQuest created.

RF. 09: Create the Credits step of the WebQuest

Registered users specify the credits in each WebQuest created.

RF. 10: Formatting WebQuest text

For each stage, all possible formatting should be reflected in the finished WebQuest.

RF. 11: Inserting images into the WebQuest

Images can be inserted into the WebQuest.

RF. 12: Formatting WebQuest images

Images inserted into the WebQuest can be formatted.

RF. 13: Creating tables in WebQuest

Tables can be inserted into the WebQuest.

RF. 14: Inserting tables into WebQuest

Tables created in WebQuest can be formatted.

RF. 15: Inserting hyperlinks in the WebQuest

Hyperlinks can be inserted into the WebQuest.

RF. 16: Formatting hyperlinks in WebQuest

Hyperlinks inserted in the WebQuest can be formatted.

RF. 17: Edit WebQuest

Registered users can edit their WebQuests.

RF. 17: Consult WebQuest

Registered users can consult their WebQuests.

RF. 18: Remove WebQuests

Registered users can remove their WebQuests at any time.

RF. 19: Close session

Registered users can leave the system at any time during the current session.

RF. 20: Produce WebQuests with all the steps

The editor should be made up of all the structural topics: introduction, task, resources, process, evaluation, conclusion and credits.

4.1.2 Non-Functional Requirements

The specification of non-functional requirements was also carried out with the support of a consultant professor, prioritising the quality, efficiency, usability, security and portability of the system to be developed.

RNF. 01: Software

The WebQuest editor will be a web application that will allow you to create and edit WebQuests.

RNF. 02: Product

It must be accessed via a compatible browser (Internet Explorer, Firefox or Chrome) as a visitor or user using a previously registered login and password.

RNF. 03: Organisation

The DAO and VO design patterns will be used to develop the editor and the Client-Server model will be used to manage the system's information.

RNF. 04: Facility

The WebQuest editor will be user-friendly with an interface based on usability principles.

RNF. 05: Efficiency

The system will generate the WebQuest as designed by the user.

RNF. 06: Reliability

The system will only be open to registered users with a login and password.

RNF. 07: Portability

The WebQuest editor can be used on any operating system with Internet access and a browser that supports HTML5.

RNF. 08: Implementation

The WebQuest editor must be developed in the PHP programming language using the DAO and VO design patterns. The application must be hosted on a web server with a MySQL database.

RNF. 09: Ethics

The system will not show users any private data.

RNF. 10: Legal

The system must comply with legal regulations, such as standards, laws and the use of intellectual property.

RNF. 11: Integration

The editor integrates with the web server, the MySQL database and the browser on the client machine.

4.1.3 Use Case Diagram

The WebQuest editor has only one actor interacting with the system (user), and this actor can carry out various operations as can be seen in Figure 4.1. The actor can register a user (with valid data) and then log in to the system (with a valid login and password) and create, edit and remove WebQuests.

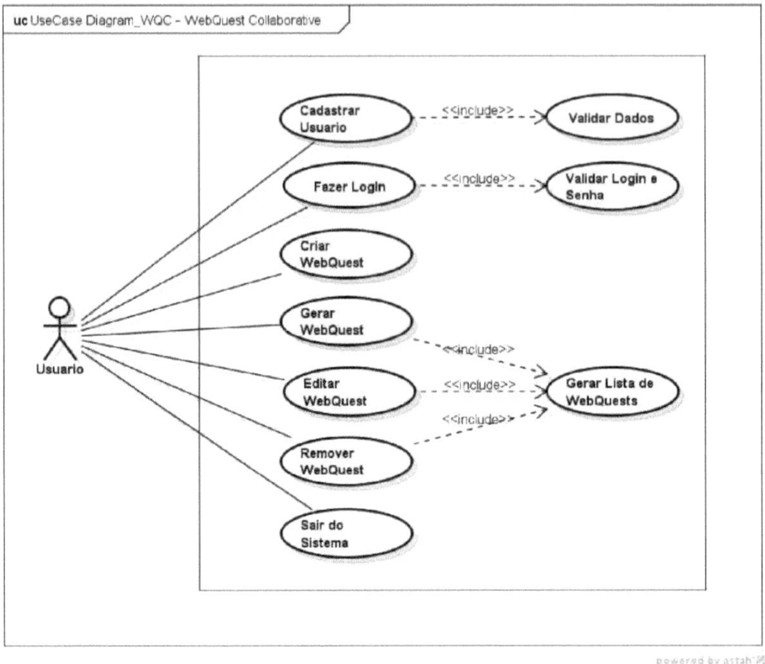

Figure 4.1 - Use Case Diagram
Source: Prepared by the author

4.1.4 ER Model

The system has a database where users save all the WebQuests created during their activity with the editor. The database stores information on user registration and the documents produced. Figure 4.2 shows the modelling of the bd-webquest database, showing both the entities with their respective relationships and the columns in each table of the project.

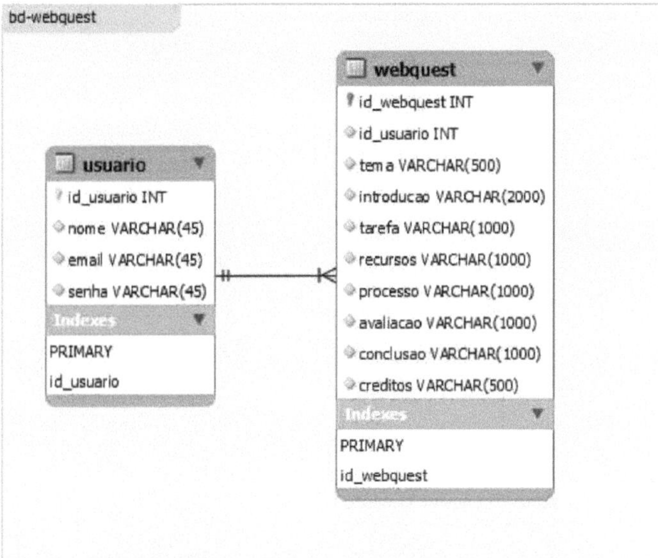

Figure 4.2 - ER model of WQC - WebQuest Collaborative

Source: Prepared by the author

4.1.5 Class Diagram

Figure 4.3 shows the software's Class Diagram, displaying both the attributes of each class and the relationships between the objects throughout the system's execution.

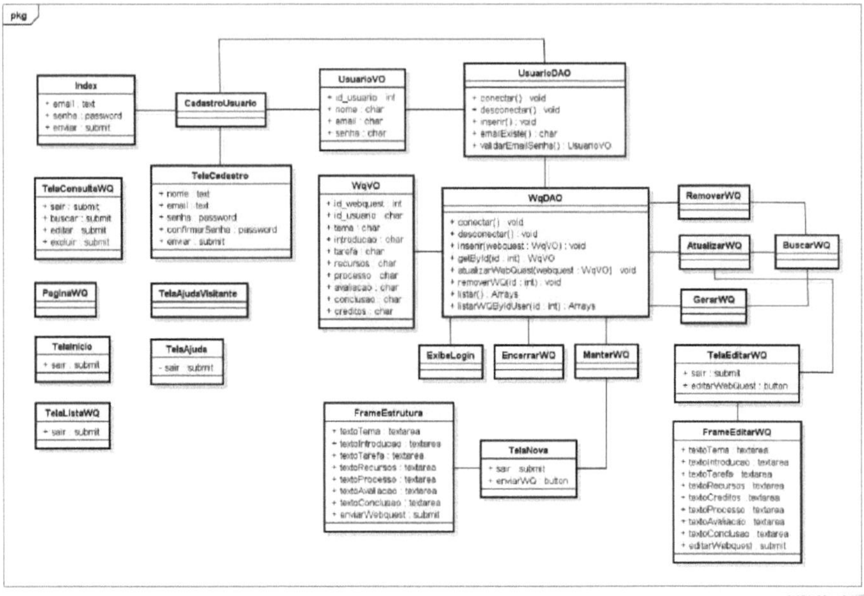

Figura 4.3 - WQC Class Diagram - WebQuest Collaborative

Source: Prepared by the author

4.1.6 Component diagram

The system's architecture is divided into three parts (system screens, system model and database). **Figure 4.4** shows these divisions in detail using the Component Diagram. The first part corresponds to the system screens, i.e. all the files related to the interface, the second part deals with the system model, includes all the files responsible for managing the database and providing the execution of the operations requested by the user and made available by the system, and the third and final part covers the system database.

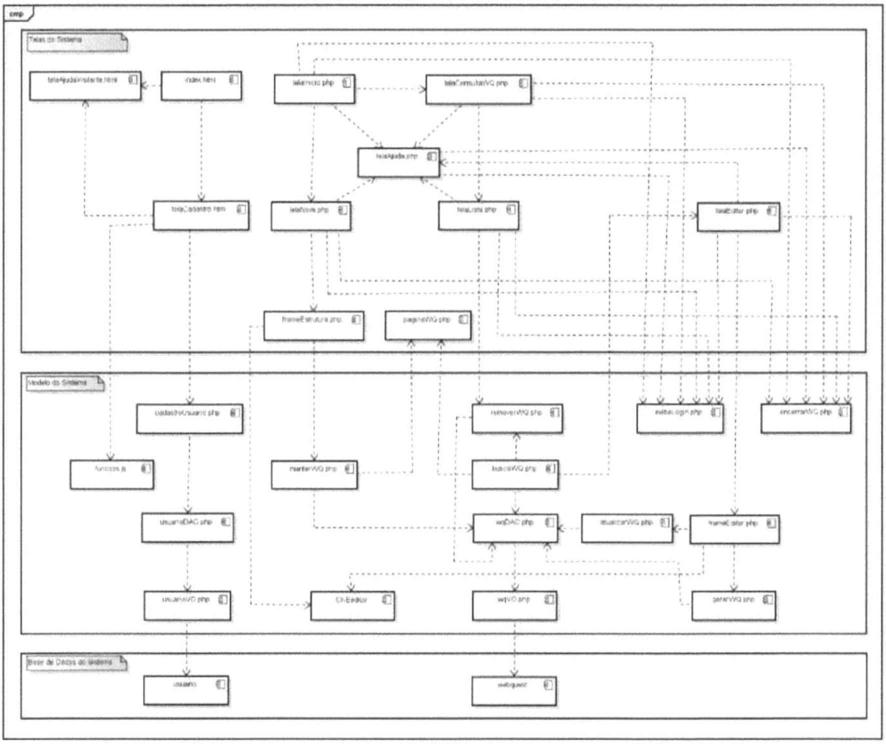

Figure 4.4 - WQC - WebQuest Collaborative Component Diagram
Source: Prepared by the author

4.2 Features

The editor's initial screen shows an area for accessing the system, a menu comprising a REGISTRATION tab (for registering new users) and a HELP tab (brief explanation of how to access the system), as can be seen in Figure 4.5, Figure 4.6 and Figure 4.7. Once registered, the visitor becomes a user of the tool and has full access by providing a valid, previously registered login and password. The system provides only one type of permission, meaning that all users can carry out all the operations allowed by the software.

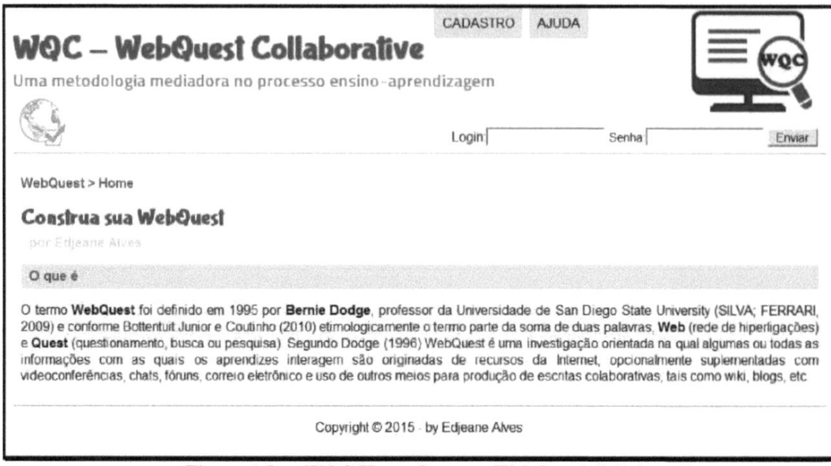

Figura 4.5 - WQC Home Screen - WebQuest Collaborative
Source: Prepared by the author

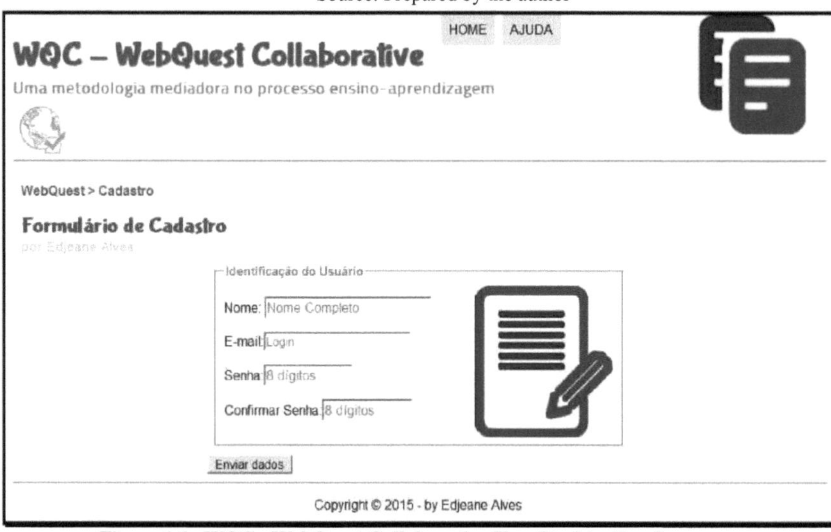

Figure 4.6 - WQC - WebQuest Collaborative User Registration Screen
Source: Prepared by the author

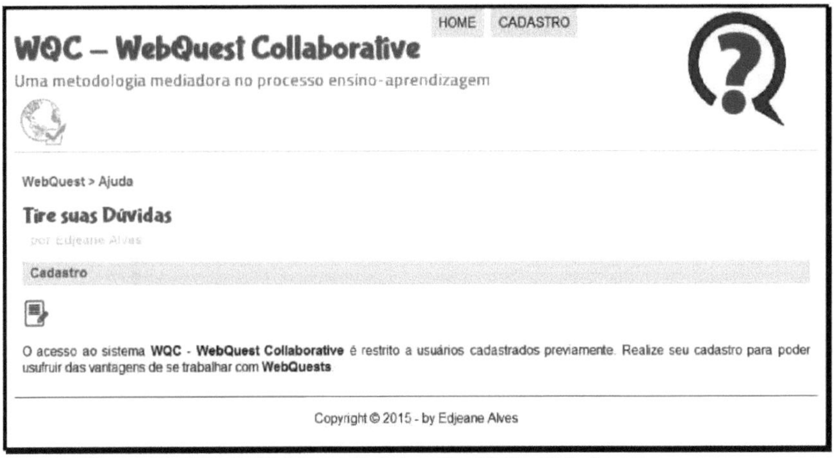

Figure 4.7 - WQC - WebQuest Collaborative Visitor Help Screen
Source: Prepared by the author

Once logged in, the user will have all the system's functions at their disposal. On the Home screen they will find the menu with the NEW, SEARCH and HELP tabs illustrated in Figure 4.8. The NEW tab allows the creation of a new WebQuest (Figure 4.9), starting with the definition of the topic to be covered and then developing each of the stages proposed by the WebQuest methodology. SEARCH takes users to a search screen (Figure 4.10) and the HELP tab provides a brief tutorial on the editor (Figure 4.12).

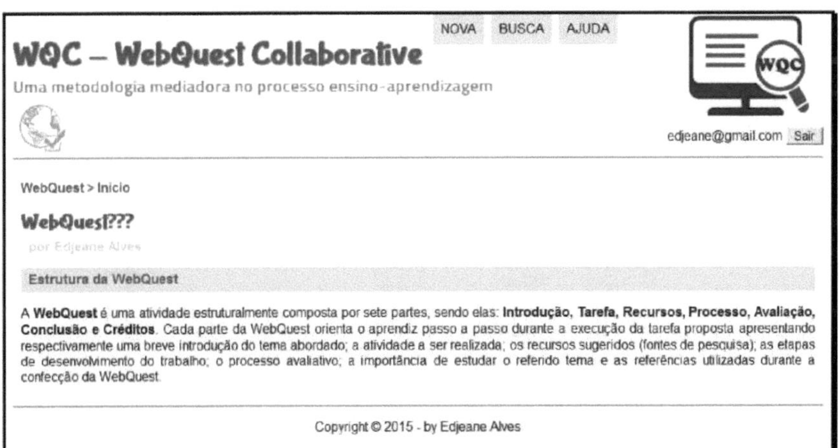

Figure 4.8 - WQC Home Screen - WebQuest Collaborative

Source: Prepared by the author

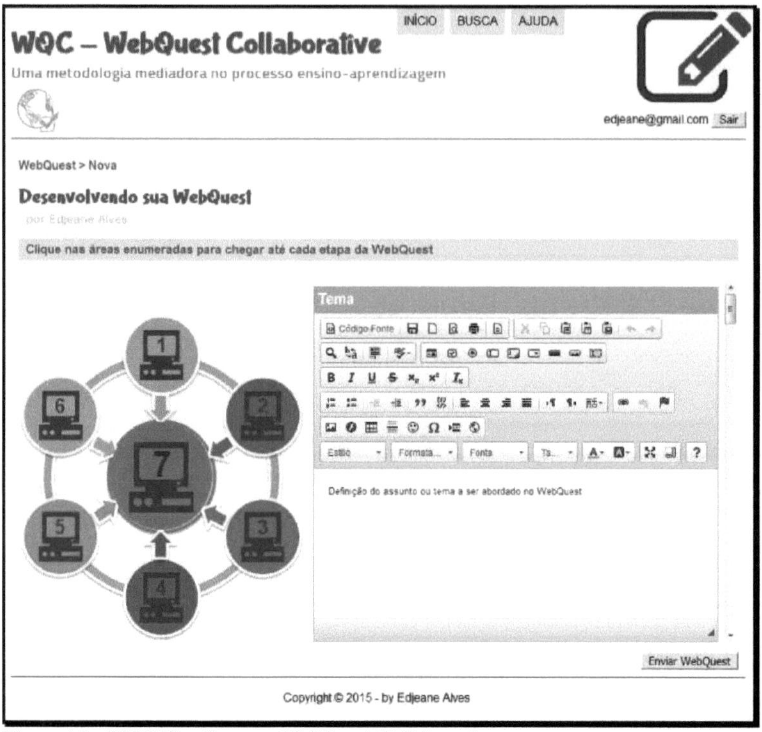

Figure 4.9 - WQC New Screen - WebQuest Collaborative
Source: Prepared by the author

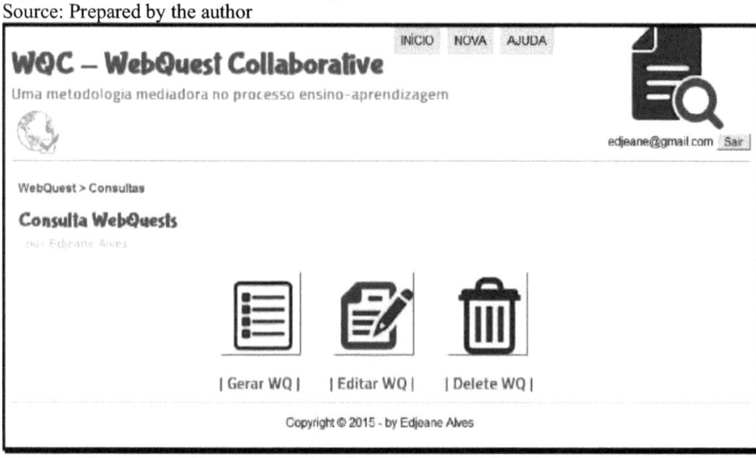

Figure 4.10 - WQC - WebQuest Collaborative enquiry screen
Source: Prepared by the author

Figure 4.11 - WQC - WebQuest Collaborative Generate WQ List Screen

Source: Prepared by the author

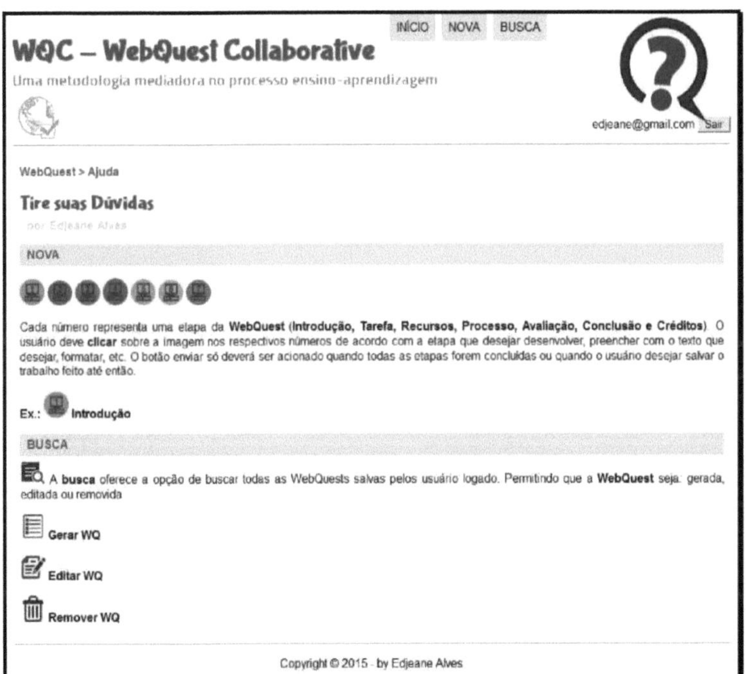

Figure 4.12 - WQC - WebQuest Collaborative User Help Screen

Source: Prepared by the author

On the queries screen (Figure 4.10), the Generate WQ, Edit WQ and Delete WQ options generate a list of all the WebQuests registered by the user. Each list generates provides a link to create a new page with the previously produced WebQuest (Figure 4.13), a link to edit the document and a link to delete a saved WebQuest. Figure 4.11 shows the list generated by the Generate WQ option.

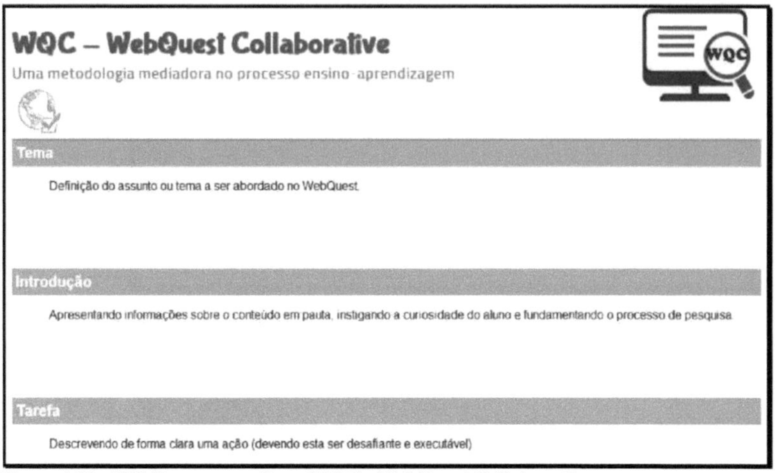

Figure 4.13 - WQ Page screen from WQC - WebQuest Collaborative

Source: Prepared by the author

CHAPTER 5

Conclusion

The WQC - WebQuest Collaborative editor is a free, open-source tool in Portuguese.

It makes it available for educators to create and edit WebQuests, emphasising their application in a collaborative way, but leaving it up to the teacher to carry out the tasks in a different way to that suggested. In this way, the use of the WebQuest editor by educators optimises collaborative activities with their students.

The web system provided has an intuitive and easy-to-use interface, meeting the needs of users and with the general aim of encouraging teacher creativity. The software can make the activities clear and objective for the students, based on differentiated lessons and in an innovative way. The tool also enhances educational resources and brings students closer to research, due to the use of Internet resources proposed in the WebQuest methodology.

The WebQuest editor brings teachers into the field of technology by bringing them closer to their students through the use of resources from this field, providing connectivity with the current world and mutual satisfaction during the teaching-learning process, given that most students are attracted to technological means in general.

WebQuest has emerged as an alternative to the collective activities proposed in the classroom, promoting the diffusion of information technologies in the school environment and consequently bringing attractiveness through the use of these media. It is therefore hoped that the results obtained will be positive in terms of the practicality, efficiency and performance of the software being used to develop collaborative work.

As future work, the suggestion is to carry out a more in-depth validation, with tests involving a significant sample of teachers, so that they use the system and answer questionnaires after use, then the data collected will be processed and the results quantified in percentages, according to the size of the defined sample.

BIBLIOGRAPHICAL REFERENCES

ABAR, Celina A. A. P.; BARBOSA, Lisbete Madsen. **Webquest um desafio para o professor: uma solução inteligente para o uso da internet**. São Paulo: Avercamp, 2008.

ALONSO, Cleuza; RIZZI, Claudia Brandelero; SEIXAS, Louise. EquiText software: a tool for collaborative writing on the Web. **VIII Taller Internacional de Software Educativo**, 2003.

ARENDT, Ronald João Jacques. Constructivism or constructionism? Contributions of this debate to Social Psychology. **Estudos de Psicologia**, v. 8, n. 1, p. 5-13, 2003.

BARRETO, Maurício Vivas de Souza. **PHP Language Course**, 2000. Available at: <http://www.etelg.com.br/paginaete/downloads/informatica/php.pdf>. Accessed on 07 August 2015.

BOTTENTUIT JUNIOR, João Batista; COUTINHO, Clara Pereira. The Use of the WebQuest Strategy in Higher Education: an analysis of two experiences. **Revista Novas Tecnologias na Educação (RENOTE)**, v. 8, n. 3. 2010.

CAELUM. **FJ 11 - Java and Object Orientation.** Available at: <https://www.caelum.com.br/download/caelum-java-objetos-fj11.pdf>. Accessed on: 02 July 2015.

CAELUM. **FJ 21 - Java for Web Development.** Available at: <https://www.caelum.com.br/download/caelum-java-web-fj21.pdf>. Accessed on: 21 June 2015.

CAMARGO, Elisa Zaroni; FERNANDES, Clovis Torres. WQE: A Versatile WebQuest Editor. In: **Proceedings of the Brazilian Symposium on Informatics in Education**. 2010.

CARDOSO, Olga Ennela Bastos de; BORGES, Eliane Medeiros. Application of the Webquest Methodology in Distance Higher Education in the Pedagogy/UAB Course at the Federal University of Juiz de Fora. **ESUD 2013 - X Brazilian Congress of Distance Higher Education Belém/PA**. Networked University Association (UniRede). 2013.

CKEditor. Available at: <http://ckeditor.com> Accessed on: 26 September 2015.

CYBIS, Walter; BETIOL, Adriana Holtz; FAUST, Richard. Ergonomics and usability. **São Paulo: Novatec**, 2010.

DELORS, Jacques et al. Report for UNESCO of the International Commission on Education for the 21st Century. **Education: a treasure to be discovered. São Paulo: UNESCO**, 1999.

DIGITAL BUSH. **Masked input plugin**. [S.l.], 2015. Available at: <http://digitalbush.com/projects/masked-input-plugin>. Accessed on: 26 September 2015.

DODGE, Bernie. **Webquest: a technique for learning on the Internet**, v. 17, p. 10-13, 2003.

DODGE, Bernie. WebQuests: **A technique for Internet -Based Learning. The Distance Educator.** Translation by Jarbas Novelino Barato. v. 1, n. 2, 1995.

FRANCO, Fábio Vilela. **COLAB-Collaborative Tool for Co-authoring Texts via the Web**. 2003.

IMS Global Consortium (2003) "IMS Learning Design Specifications". Available at: <http://www.imsglobal.org/learningdesign/>. Accessed on: 13 September 2015.

NETO, J. S.; PASSARO, A.; FERNANDES, C. T. Webquest as a Tool to Support Students in Learning Sensors and Actuators. **II IEAv Science and Technology Symposium**, 2014.

NEVES, Rita de Araujo; DAMIANI, Magda Floriana. **Vygotsky and learning theories**. 2006.

NIELSEN, Jakob; LORANGER, Hoa. **Usability on the web**. Elsevier Brazil, 2007.

PALANGANA, Isilda Campaner. **Development and learning in Piaget and Vygotsky: the relevance of the social**. Summus Publishing Group, 2001.

PASSERINO, Liliana Maria; SANTAROSA, Lucila Maria Costi. A socio-historical view of interaction within computer environments. In: **Proceedings of the 5th Ibero-American Congress on Informatics in Education RIBIE**. 2000. p. 3-4.

PHPWebQuest - Project Site (2009). Available at:< http://phpwebquest.org>. Accessed on: 26 September 2015.

PHPWebQuest in Portuguese (2008). Available at: <http://www.webquestbrasil.org/node/9>. Accessed on: 26 September 2015.

SANCHO, Juana Maria. [et al.]; translated by Valério Campos. **Technologies for transforming education.** Porto Alegre: Artmed, 2006.

SANTOS, Camila Gonçalves dos. **The Webquest Dob Methodology in the Light of Activity Theory: a Proposal**. 2012.

SANTOS, Leila Maria Araújo; TAROUCO, Liane Margarida Rockenbach. The importance of studying cognitive load theory in technological education. **Revista Novas Tecnologias na Educação (RENOTE)**, v. 5, n. 1, 2007.

SILVA, Fernanda Quaresma da; FERRARI, Hélio Oliveira. Webquest as a didactic activity that enhances education. **Revista Novas Tecnologias na Educação (RENOTE)**, v. 7, n. 1, 2009.

TAROUCO, Liane Margarida Rockenbach; CUNHA, Silvio Luiz Souza. Applying cognitive theories to the design of learning objects. **Revista Novas Tecnologias na Educação (RENOTE)**, v. 4, n. 2, 2006.

TORRES, Elisabeth Fátima; MAZZONI, Alberto Angel. Multimedia digital content: the focus on usability and accessibility. **Ci. Inf., Brasília**, v. 33, n. 2, p. 152-160, 2004.

VIEIRA, Yauari. **Webquester: Tool for Creating Webquest with Online Assessments**. 2008.

VYGOTSKY, L.S. Thought and language. São Paulo: Martins Fontes, 1989.

WINCKLER, Marco; PIMENTA, Marcelo Soares. Website usability evaluation. **Escola de Informática da SBC SUL (ERI 2002) ed. Porto Alegre: Sociedade Brasileira de Computação (SBC)**, v. 1, p. 85-137, 2002.

ZANK, Cláudia. **Collective text editor (CTE) contributions to the development of teamwork competences.** 2010.

ZEND. **Zend studio**: the proven PHP development environment. [California], 2015. Available at: <http://www.zend.com/products/zend_studio>. Accessed on: 26 September 2015.

ZUNAL. Available at: <http://www.zunal.com>. Accessed on: 26 September 2015.

APPENDIX A - Detailed Use Cases

Use case name	Register User
General use case	
Main actor	Visitor
Secondary actors	
Summary	Describes the steps required to register a user in the system.
Preconditions	
Post - Conditions	
Main Flow	
Actor's actions	**System Actions**
1. Request the registration option.	
	2. Display the registration screen.
3. Enter the user's full name.	
4. Enter a valid e-mail address for login.	
5. Create an 8-digit password.	
6. Confirm password.	
	7. Check that the e-mail is valid.
	8. Check that the e-mail address is already linked to a system account.
	9. Check that the password has 8 or more digits.
	10. Check that the passwords entered are the same.
	11. Register User.

Exception Flow001: Invalid e-mail	
	1. In step 7 of the Main Flow, the system identified that the e-mail entered was invalid.
	2. Inform them that their e-mail address is invalid.
Exception Flow 002: Existing e-mail	
	1. In step 8 of the Main Flow, the system identified that the e-mail address entered had already been registered.
	2. Inform them that the e-mail address entered has already been registered.
Exception Flow 003: Password shorter than 8 digits	
	1. In step 9 of the Main Flow, the system identified that the password entered has less than 8 digits.
	3. Inform them that the password must have 8 or more digits.
Exception Flow 003: Different passwords	
	1. In step 10 of the Main Flow, the system identified that the passwords entered were different.
	4. Inform them that the passwords must be the same.

Use case name	Login
General use case	
Main actor	User
Secondary actors	
Summary	Describes the steps required for the user to access the system.
Preconditions	
Post - Conditions	
Main Flow	
Actor's actions	**System Actions**
1. log in.	
2. Enter your password.	
3. Request access.	
	4. Verify login and password.
	5. Log in.
	6. Display the start screen.
Exception Flow 001: Incorrect login and/or password	
	1. In step 2 of the Main Flow, the system identified that the login and/or password entered were incorrect.
	2. Inform them that their login and/or password is incorrect.

Use case name	Create WebQuest
General use case	
Main actor	User
Secondary actors	

Summary	Describes the steps needed to create a WebQuest.
Preconditions	
Post - Conditions	
Main Flow	
Actor's actions	**System Actions**
1. Request the New WebQuest option.	
	2. Display *the* screen needed to create a new WebQuest.
3. Type in the topic to be covered, the introduction, the task, the resources, the process, the evaluation, the conclusion and the credits for the WebQuest.	
	4. Check that all the steps have been completed.
	5. Create a new WebQuest.
Exception Flow 001: Stage not completed	
	1. In step *P* of the Main Flow, the system has identified that one of the WebQuest steps has not been completed.
	2. Inform them that the WebQuest will not be created.

Use case name	Generate WebQuest
General use case	
Main actor	User
Secondary actors	
Summary	Describes the steps needed to generate a WebQuest.
Preconditions	
Post - Conditions	
Main Flow	
Actor's actions	**System Actions**
1. Request the Generate WebQuest option.	
	2. Generate a list of all the WebQuests registered by the user.
3. Select the WebQuest to be generated.	
	4. Generate WebQuest.
	5. Display a new page with the generated WebQuest.
Exception Flow 001: Stage not completed	
	1. In step 4 of the Main Flow
	system has identified that one of the WebQuest steps has not been completed.
	2. Inform them that the WebQuest will not be edited.

Use case name	Edit WebQuest
General use case	
Main actor	User
Secondary actors	

Summary	Describes the steps needed to edit a WebQuest.
Preconditions	
Post - Conditions	
Main Flow	
Actor's actions	**System Actions**
2. Request the Edit WebQuest option.	
	3. Generate a list of all the WebQuests registered by the user.
4. Select the WebQuest to be edited.	
	6. Display the screen needed to edit the WebQuest.
7. Make changes to the WebQuest steps.	
	8. Check that all the steps of the WebQuest have been completed.
	9. Edit WebQuest.
Exception Flow 001: Stage not completed	
	3. In step *p of* the Main Flow, the system has identified that one of theof the WebQuest was not filled.
	4. Inform them that the WebQuest will not be edited.

Use case name	Remove WebQuest
General use case	
Main actor	User
Secondary actors	
Summary	Describes the steps needed to remove a WebQuest.
Preconditions	
Post - Conditions	
Main Flow	
Actor's actions	**System Actions**
3. Request the Delete WebQuest option.	
	4. Generate a list of all the WebQuests registered by the user.
5. Select the WebQuest to be removed.	
	10. Remove WebQuest.

Use case name	Exit the system
General use case	
Main actor	User
Secondary actors	
Summary	Describes the steps required for the user to exit the system.
Preconditions	
Post - Conditions	
Main Flow	
Actor's actions	**System Actions**
1. Ask to leave the system.	
	2. Close the session.

	3. Exit the system.

APPENDIX B - Verification of Requirements

RF. 01	**Register users**
Requirements Related	None
Test objective:	Ensure proper functionality of the test target, including navigation, data entry, processing and retrieval.
Technique:	Execute use case, use case flow, using valid and invalid data, to check the following: ▪ Expected results occur when valid data is used; ▪ The appropriate error or warning messages are displayed when invalid data is used; ▪ Each business rule is applied appropriately.
Criteria Finalisation:	▪ All the planned tests were carried out. ▪ All the defects identified have been dealt with.
Considerations Specials:	None

RF. 02	**Create the WebQuest Theme step**
Requirements Related	None
Test objective:	Ensure proper functionality of the test target, including navigation, data entry, processing, and retrieval.
Technique:	Execute use case, use case flow, using valid and invalid data, to check the following: ▪ The expected results occur when the field is filled in; ▪ The appropriate error messages or warnings are displayed when the field is not filled in; ▪ Each business rule is applied appropriately.
Criteria Finalisation:	▪ All the planned tests were carried out. ▪ All the defects identified have been dealt with.
Considerations Specials:	None

RF. 03	**Create the Introduction stage of the WebQuest**
Requirements Related	None
Test objective:	Ensure proper functionality of the test target, including navigation, data entry, processing, and retrieval.
Technique:	Execute use case, use case flow, using valid and invalid data, to check the following: ▪ The expected results occur when the field is filled in; ▪ The appropriate error messages or warnings are displayed when the field is not filled in; ▪ Each business rule is applied appropriately.
Criteria Finalisation:	▪ All the planned tests were carried out. ▪ All the defects identified have been dealt with.
Considerations Specials:	None

RF. 04	**Create the WebQuest Task step**
Requirements Related	None
Test objective:	Ensure proper functionality of the test target, including navigation, data entry, processing, and retrieval.
Technique:	Execute use case, use case flow, using valid and invalid data, to check the following: ▪ The expected results occur when the field is filled in; ▪ The appropriate error messages or warnings are displayed when the field is not filled in; ▪ Each business rule is applied appropriately.
Criteria Finalisation:	▪ All the planned tests were carried out. ▪ All the defects identified have been dealt with.
Considerations Specials:	None

RF. 05	**Create the WebQuest Resources step**
Requirements Related	None
Test objective:	Ensure proper functionality of the test target, including navigation, data entry, processing, and retrieval.
Technique:	Execute use case, use case flow, using valid and invalid data, to check the following: ▪ The expected results occur when the field is filled in; ▪ The appropriate error messages or warnings are displayed when the field is not filled in; ▪ Each business rule is applied appropriately.
Criteria Finalisation:	▪ All the planned tests were carried out. ▪ All the defects identified have been dealt with.
Considerations Specials:	None

RF. 06	**Create the WebQuest Process step**
Requirements Related	None
Test objective:	Ensure proper functionality of the test target, including navigation, data entry, processing, and retrieval.
Technique:	Execute use case, use case flow, using valid data and invalid , to check the following: ▪ The expected results occur when the field is filled in; ▪ The appropriate error messages or warnings are displayed when the field is not filled in; ▪ Each business rule is applied appropriately.
Criteria Finalisation:	▪ All the planned tests were carried out. ▪ All the defects identified have been dealt with.
Special Considerations:	None

RF. 07	**Create the WebQuest Evaluation step**
Requirements Related	None
Test objective:	Ensure proper functionality of the test target, including navigation, data

	entry, processing, and retrieval.
Technique:	Execute use case, use case flow, using valid and invalid data, to check the following: ■ The expected results occur when the field is filled in; ■ The appropriate error messages or warnings are displayed when the field is not filled in; ■ Each business rule is applied appropriately.
Criteria Finalisation:	■ All the planned tests were carried out. ■ All the defects identified have been dealt with.
Special Considerations:	None

RF. 08	**Create the WebQuest Conclusion step**
Requirements Related	None
Test objective:	Ensure proper functionality of the test target, including navigation, data entry, processing, and retrieval.
Technique:	Execute use case, use case flow, using valid and invalid data, to check the following: ■ The expected results occur when the field is filled in; ■ The appropriate error messages or warnings are displayed when the field is not filled in; ■ Each business rule is applied appropriately.
Criteria Finalisation:	■ All the planned tests were carried out. ■ All the defects identified have been dealt with.
Considerations Specials:	None

RF. 09	**Create the WebQuest Credits step**
Requirements Related	None
Test objective:	Ensure proper functionality of the test target, including navigation, data entry, processing, and retrieval.
Technique:	Execute use case, use case flow, using valid and invalid data, to check the following: ■ The expected results occur when the field is filled in; ■ The appropriate error messages or warnings are displayed when the field is not filled in; ■ Each business rule is applied appropriately.
Criteria Finalisation:	■ All the planned tests were carried out. ■ All the defects identified have been dealt with.
Special Considerations:	None

RF. 10	**Formatting WebQuest text**
Requirements Related	None
Test objective:	Ensure proper functionality of the test target, including navigation, data entry, processing, and retrieval.
Technique:	Execute use case, use case flow, using valid and invalid commands, to check the following: ■ The expected results occur when formatting is requested;

	■ The appropriate error or warning messages are displayed when unauthorised changes are made; ■ Each business rule is applied appropriately.
Criteria Finalisation:	■ All the planned tests were carried out. ■ All the defects identified have been dealt with.
Considerations Specials:	None

RF. 11	**Inserting images into the WebQuest**
Requirements Related	None
Test objective:	Ensure proper functionality of the test target, including navigation, data entry, processing, and retrieval.
Technique:	Execute use case, use case flow, using valid and invalid commands, to check the following: ■ The expected results occur when the image is positioned. ■ Each business rule is applied appropriately.
Criteria Finalisation:	■ All the planned tests were carried out. ■ All the defects identified have been dealt with.
Considerations Specials:	None

RF. 12	**Formatting images in WebQuest**
Requirements Related	None
Test objective:	Ensure proper functionality of the test target, including navigation, data entry, processing, and retrieval.
Technique:	Execute use case, use case flow, using valid and invalid commands, to check the following: ■ The expected results occur when formatting is requested; ■ The appropriate error or warning messages are displayed when unauthorised changes are made; ■ Each business rule is applied appropriately.
Criteria Finalisation:	■ All the planned tests were carried out. ■ All the defects identified have been dealt with.
Considerations Specials:	None

RF. 14	**Inserting tables in WebQuest**
Requirements Related	None
Test objective:	Ensure proper functionality of the test target, including navigation, data entry, processing, and retrieval.
Technique:	Execute use case, use case flow, using valid and invalid commands, to check the following: ■ The expected results occur when valid commands are used; ■ The appropriate error or warning messages are invalid commands are used; ■ Each business rule is applied appropriately.
Criteria Finalisation:	■ All the planned tests were carried out.

	▪ All the defects identified have been dealt with.
Considerations Specials:	None

RF. 15	**Insert hyperlink in WebQuest**
Requirements Related	None
Test objective:	Ensure proper functionality of the test target, including navigation, data entry, processing, and retrieval.
Technique:	Execute use case, use case flow, using valid and invalid data, to check the following: ▪ Expected results occur when valid data is used; ▪ The appropriate error or warning messages are displayed when invalid data is used; ▪ Each business rule is applied appropriately.
Criteria Finalisation:	▪ All the planned tests were carried out. ▪ All the defects identified have been dealt with.
Special Considerations:	None

RF. 16	**Formatting hyperlinks in WebQuest**
Requirements Related	None
Test objective:	Ensure proper functionality of the test target, including navigation, data entry, processing, and retrieval.
Technique:	Execute use case, use case flow, using valid and invalid commands, to check the following: ▪ The expected results occur when commands are used; ▪ The appropriate error or warning messages are displayed when invalid commands are used; ▪ Each business rule is applied appropriately.
Criteria Finalisation:	▪ All the planned tests were carried out. ▪ All the defects identified have been dealt with.
Special Considerations:	None

RF. 17	**Edit WebQuest**
Requirements Related	None
Test objective:	Ensure proper functionality of the test target, including navigation, data entry, processing, and retrieval.
Technique:	Execute use case, use case flow, using valid and invalid data, to check the following: ▪ Expected results occur when valid data is used; ▪ The appropriate error or warning messages are displayed when invalid data is used; ▪ Each business rule is applied appropriately.
Criteria Finalisation:	▪ All the planned tests were carried out. ▪ All the defects identified have been dealt with.
Considerations Specials:	None
RF. 17	**Consult WebQuest**
Requirements	None

Related	
Test objective:	Ensure proper functionality of the test target, including navigation, data entry, processing, and retrieval.
Technique:	Execute use case, use case flow, using valid and invalid WebQuest, to check the following: ■ The expected results occur when valid WebQuests are used; ■ The appropriate error or warning messages are displayed when invalid WebQuests are used; ■ Each business rule is applied appropriately.
Criteria Finalisation:	■ All the planned tests were carried out. ■ All the defects identified have been dealt with.
Considerations Specials:	None

RF. 18	**Remove WebQuest**
Requirements Related	None
Test objective:	Ensure proper functionality of the test target, including navigation, data entry, processing, and retrieval.
Technique:	Execute use case, use case flow, using valid and invalid WebQuest, to check the following: ■ The expected results occur when valid WebQuests are used; ■ The appropriate error or warning messages are displayed when invalid WebQuests are used; ■ Each business rule is applied appropriately.
Criteria Finalisation:	■ All the planned tests were carried out. ■ All the defects identified have been dealt with.
Considerations Specials:	None

RF. 19	**End session**
Requirements Related	None
Test objective:	Ensure proper functionality of the test target, including navigation, data entry, processing, and retrieval.
Technique:	Execute use case, use case flow, using valid and invalid requests, to check the following: ■ The expected results occur when the request is made; ■ The appropriate error or warning messages are displayed when invalid requests are used; ■ Each business rule is applied appropriately.
Criteria Finalisation:	■ All the planned tests were carried out. ■ All the defects identified have been dealt with.
Considerations Specials:	None

RF. 20	**Produce WebQuests with all the steps**
Requirements Related	None
Test objective:	Ensure proper functionality of the test target, including navigation, data entry, processing, and retrieval.

Technique:	Execute use case, use case flow, using valid and invalid data, to check the following: ■ Expected results occur when valid data is used; ■ The appropriate error or warning messages are displayed when invalid data is used; ■ Each business rule is applied appropriately.
Criteria Finalisation:	■ All the planned tests were carried out. ■ All the defects identified have been dealt with.
Considerations Specials:	None

MIX
Papier aus verantwortungsvollen Quellen
Paper from responsible sources
FSC® C105338

Printed by Books on Demand GmbH, Norderstedt / Germany